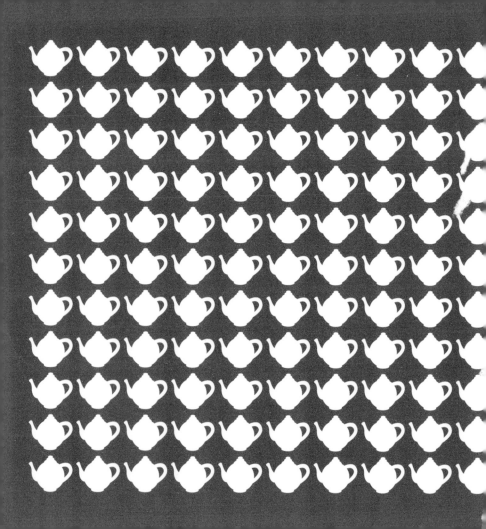

GREAT BRITAIN

LET'S GET QUIZZICAL

GWION PRYDDERCH

SUMMERSDALE PUBLISHERS LTD
46 WEST STREET
CHICHESTER
WEST SUSSEX
PO19 1RP
UK

WWW.SUMMERSDALE.COM
PRINTED AND BOUND IN CHINA
ISBN: 978-1-84953-589-2

THIS PAIR ONLY APPEARS ONCE
ON THE OPPOSITE PAGE

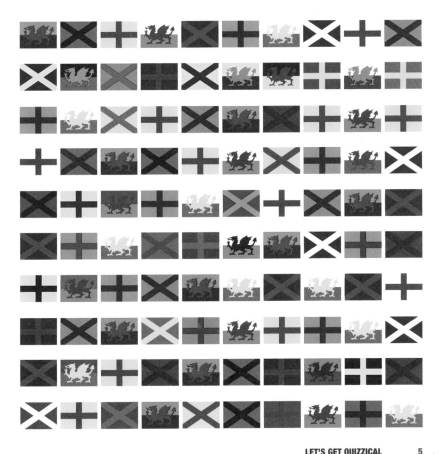

IN 1915 CECIL CHUBB BOUGHT STONEHENGE AT AUCTION FOR £6,600 AS:

A) A GIFT FOR HIS WIFE

B) GRAZING LAND FOR HIS CATTLE

C) A LOCATION FOR A PRIVATE FESTIVAL

LONDON
EDINBURGH
CARDIFF
GLASGOW
MANCHESTER
DUNDEE
BANGOR
NEWCASTLE
SWANSEA
ABERDEEN
OXFORD
CAMBRIDGE
NEWPORT
BATH

```
A B E R D E E N L M
C A L O N D O N G A
A N H X F U A E L N
M G R F F N E W A C
B O H O I D S P S H
R R T R D E N O G E
I O A D R E A R O S
D N B S A T W T W T
G N E W C A S T L E
E D I N B U R G H R
```

WHAT ARE THE NATIONAL FLOWERS OF ENGLAND, SCOTLAND AND WALES?

A) WELSH ROSE, SCOTTISH DAFFODIL, ENGLISH THISTLE

B) SCOTTISH ROSE, ENGLISH DAFFODIL, WELSH THISTLE

C) ENGLISH ROSE, WELSH DAFFODIL, SCOTTISH THISTLE

THIS PAIR ONLY APPEARS ONCE ON THE OPPOSITE PAGE

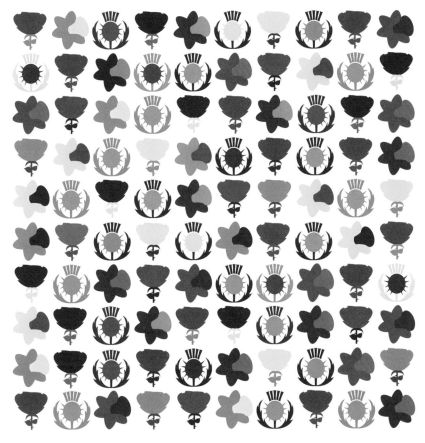

SPOT THE DIFFERENCE – THERE'S ONLY ONE!

THE ORIGINAL MINI WAS DESIGNED WITH POCKETS IN ITS DOORS, REPORTEDLY TO FIT:

A) A PAIR OF DRIVING GLOVES

B) A BOTTLE OF GORDON'S GIN

C) THE DESIGNER'S WIFE'S MAKEUP CASE

THIS PAIR ONLY APPEARS ONCE
ON THE OPPOSITE PAGE

APPROXIMATELY HOW MANY PEOPLE SEE THE ANGEL OF THE NORTH EVERY DAY?

A) 20,000

B) 90,000

C) 120,000

BRITISH RIVERS

SEVERN
THAMES
TRENT
GREAT OUSE
WYE
URE
TAY
SPEY
CLYDE
NENE
TWEED
TAFF
AVON
EDEN
DEE

R I V F F B A U S I
K T H A M E S Y P G
C R L Y E D E X E R
L E F F U E V W Y E
Y N V A D N E I J A
A T W E E D R U M T
V A Y N E F N V B O
O Y C L Y D E M E U
N L T A F F N T R S
W E R T Y U E U R E

WHICH PART OF BRITAIN HAS MORE CASTLES PER HEAD THAN ANYWHERE ELSE IN THE WORLD?

A) ENGLAND

B) SCOTLAND

C) WALES

GET BOBBY TO HIS TRUNCHEON!

HOW MANY NOTES CAN THE SCOTTISH GREAT HIGHLAND BAGPIPE PLAY?

A) 9

B) 19

C) 99

SPOT THE DIFFERENCE – THERE'S ONLY ONE!

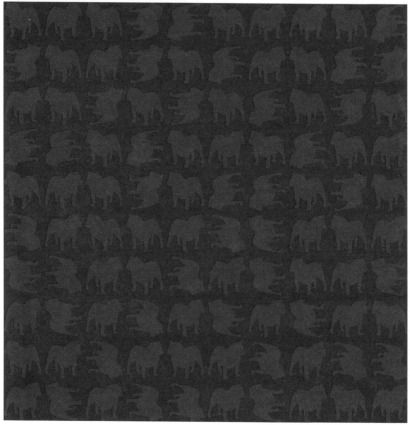

APART FROM IN A BATHROOM, WHERE CAN A PREGNANT WOMAN IN BRITAIN LEGALLY RELIEVE HERSELF?

A) IN A CHURCH

B) IN A POLICE STATION

C) ANYWHERE SHE WISHES

GET MORRIS TO HIS MAYPOLE!

WHERE IS THE UNION JACK BUTTERFLY *(DELIAS MYSIS)* FROM?

A) ENGLAND

B) CHINA

C) AUSTRALIA

SPOT THE DIFFERENCE – THERE'S ONLY ONE!

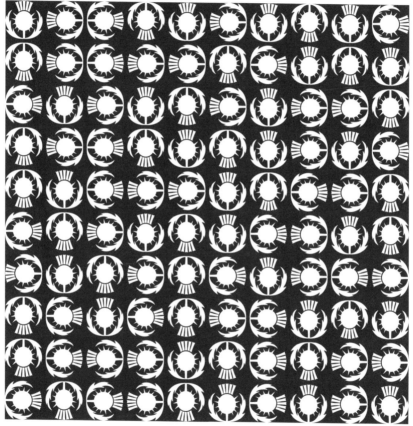

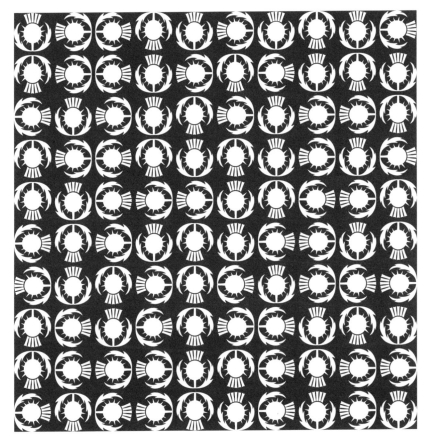

APPROXIMATELY HOW MANY PEOPLE IN WALES ARE ABLE TO SPEAK WELSH?

A) 180,000

B) 330,000

C) 560,000

THIS PAIR ONLY APPEARS ONCE
ON THE OPPOSITE PAGE

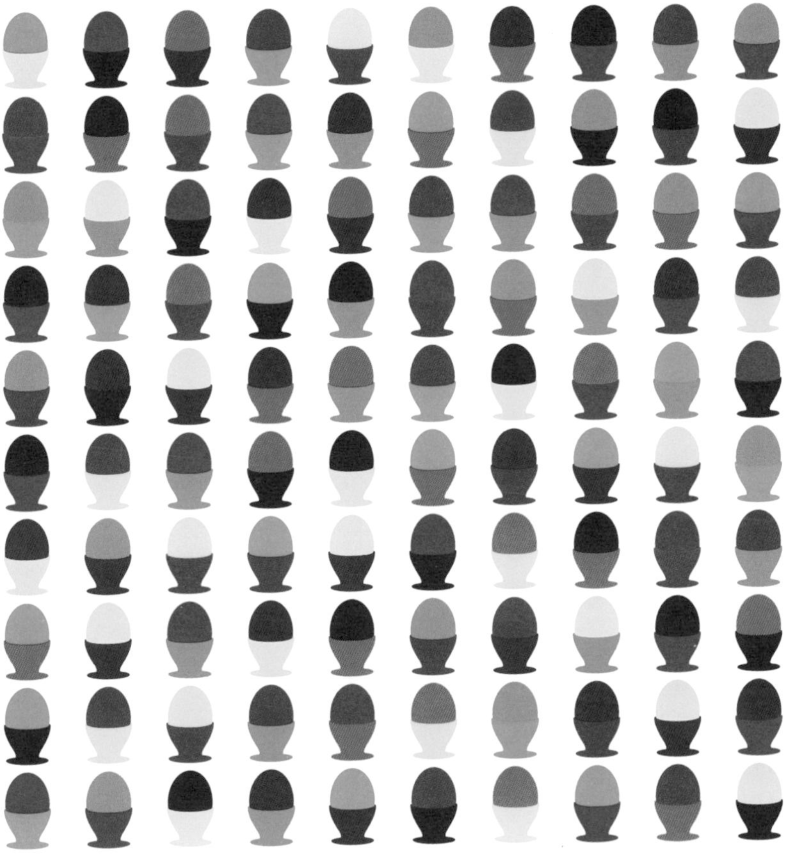

IN 1592 IT WAS FORBIDDEN TO SELL HOT CROSS BUNS EXCEPT DURING?

A) BURIALS, GOOD FRIDAY AND CHRISTMAS

B) SUNDAY AND WEDNESDAY

C) WEDDINGS AND CHRISTENINGS

 **FIND THE BLUE SEAGULL**

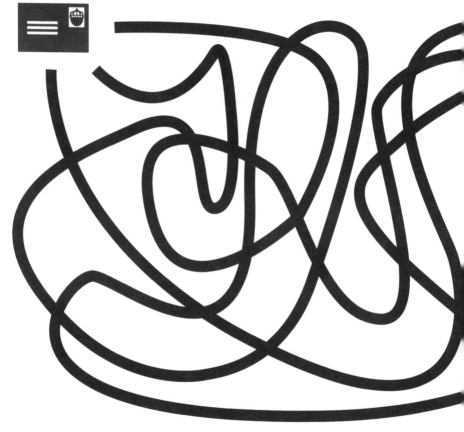

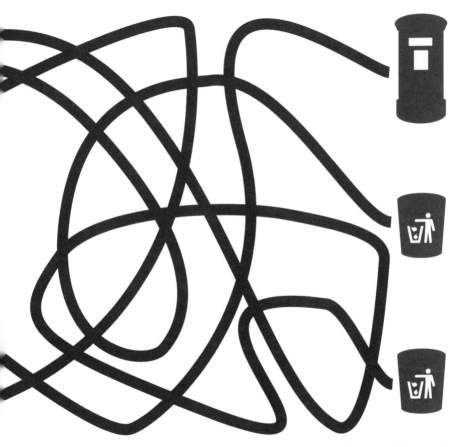

LLANFAIRPWLLGWYNGYLLGOGERYCHW

THIS VILLAGE ON THE ISLAND OF ANGLESEY IN WALES HAS THE LONGEST PLACE NAME IN EUROPE, BUT WHERE ELSE HAS IT BEEN USED?

YRNDROBWLLLLANTYSILIOGOGOGOCH

A) AS THE ADDRESS OF JAMES BOND'S ENEMY IN *GOLDFINGER*

B) AS THE NAME OF THE DALEKS' HIDEOUT IN *DR WHO*

C) AS THE PASSWORD FOR THE HEADQUARTERS OF DILDANO IN THE MOVIE *BARBARELLA*

THIS PAIR ONLY APPEARS ONCE ON THE OPPOSITE PAGE

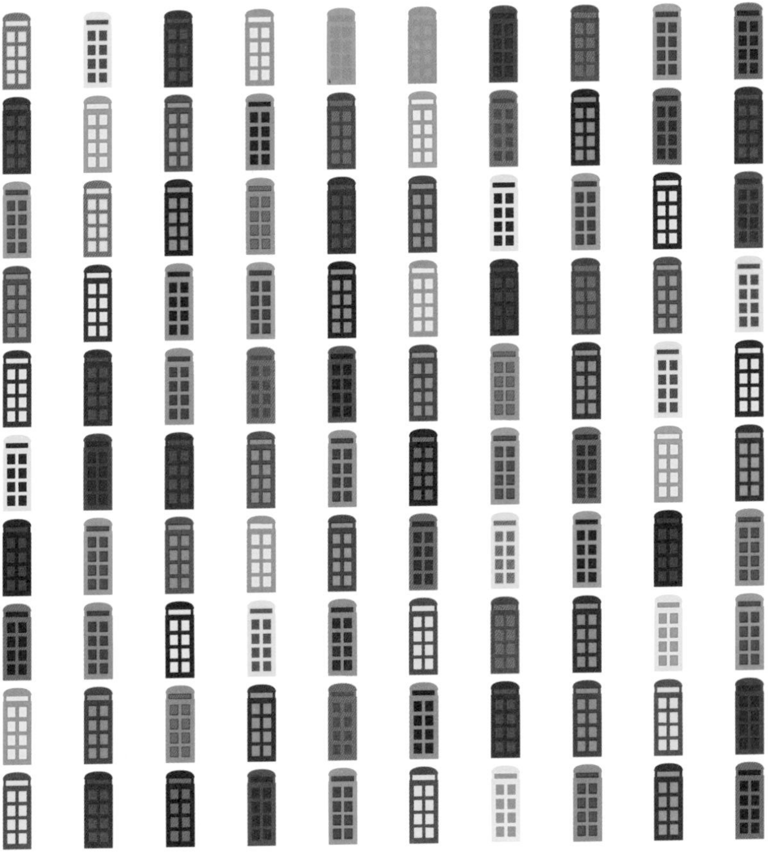

ACCORDING TO THE RULES OF HAGGIS HURLING – A SCOTTISH SPORT WHERE A HAGGIS IS THROWN – WHAT MUST THE HAGGIS BE AFTER LANDING?

A) FACING NORTH

B) EDIBLE

C) ON ITS BACK

BRITISH MOUNTAINS

BEN NEVIS
SNOWDON
LIATHACH
SCAFELL PIKE
GOAT FELL
PEN Y FAN
LOCHNAGAR
CROSS FELL
GLYDER FAWR

```
L I A T H A C H C G
L O C H N A G A R L
G O A T F E L L O Y
R S N O W D O N S D
A C A J K R W I S E
T A F A P E R G F R
C F Y U L A S D E F
B E N N E V I S L A
O L E H F P O I L W
R L P I K E W Y N R
```

SPOT THE DIFFERENCE – THERE'S ONLY ONE!

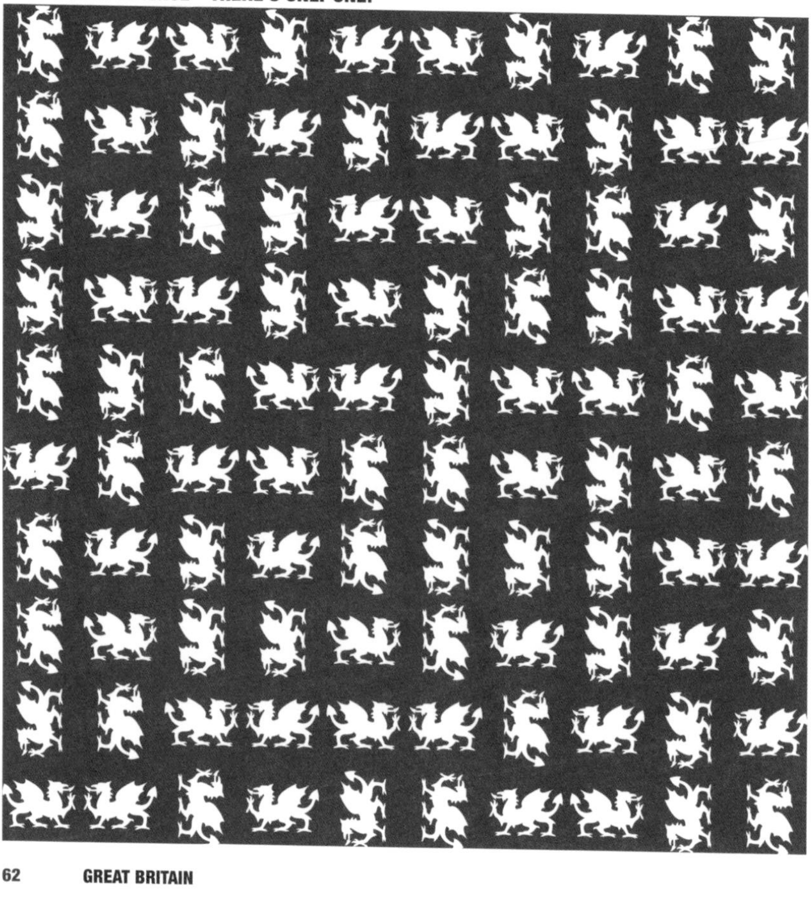

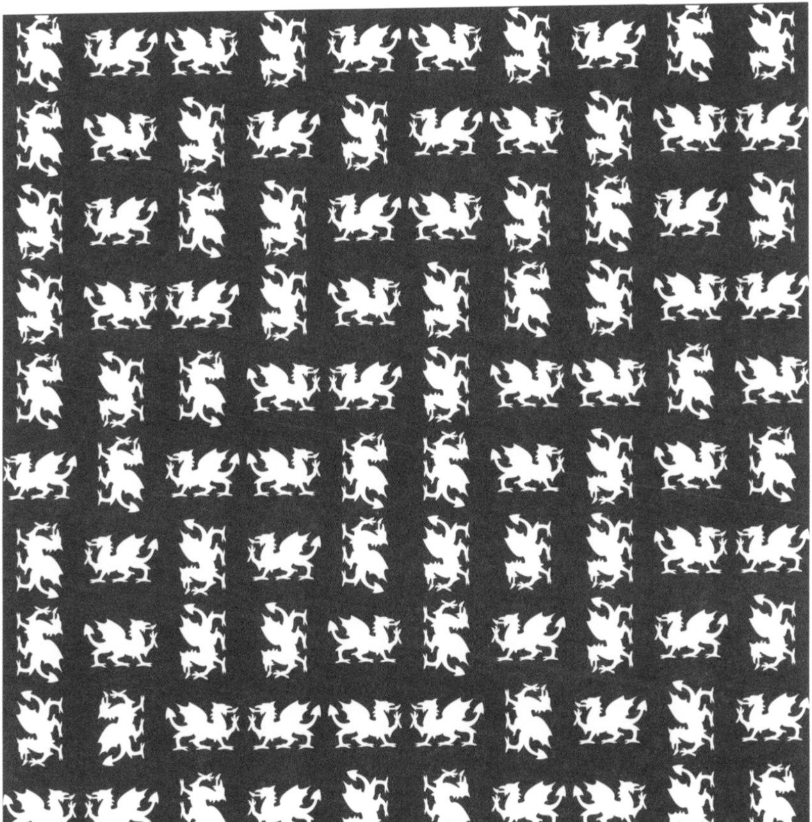

THIS PAIR ONLY APPEARS ONCE
ON THE OPPOSITE PAGE

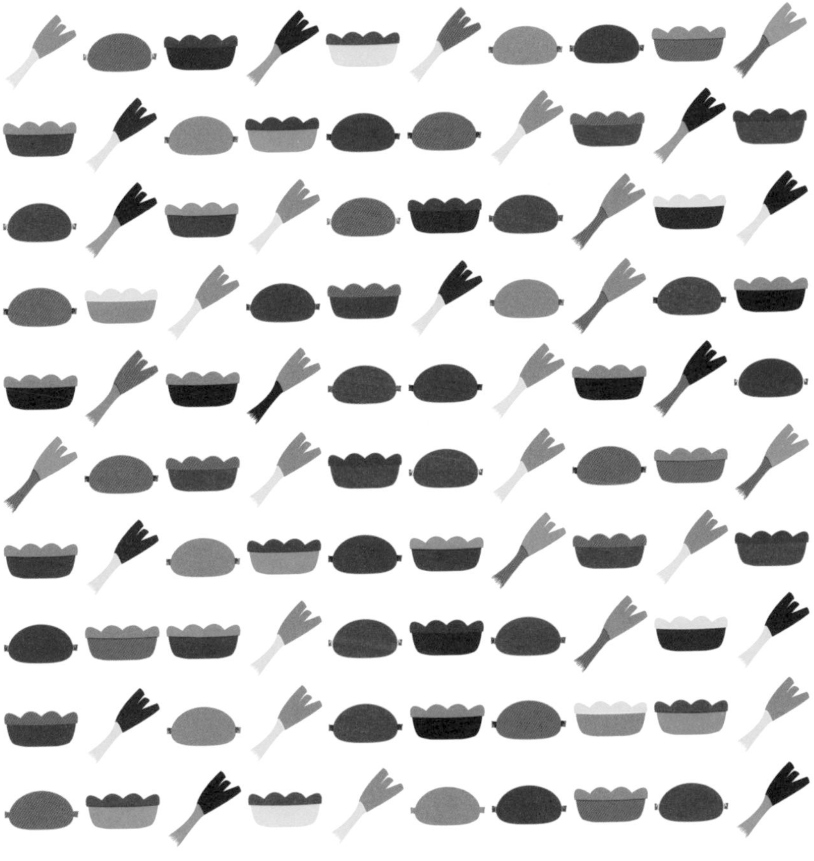

HOW MUCH METAL WAS USED IN THE CONSTRUCTION OF THE FORTH RAIL BRIDGE IN SCOTLAND?

A) TWICE AS MUCH AS THE EIFFEL TOWER

B) TEN TIMES AS MUCH

C) FIFTEEN TIMES AS MUCH

THIS PAIR ONLY APPEARS ONCE ON THE OPPOSITE PAGE

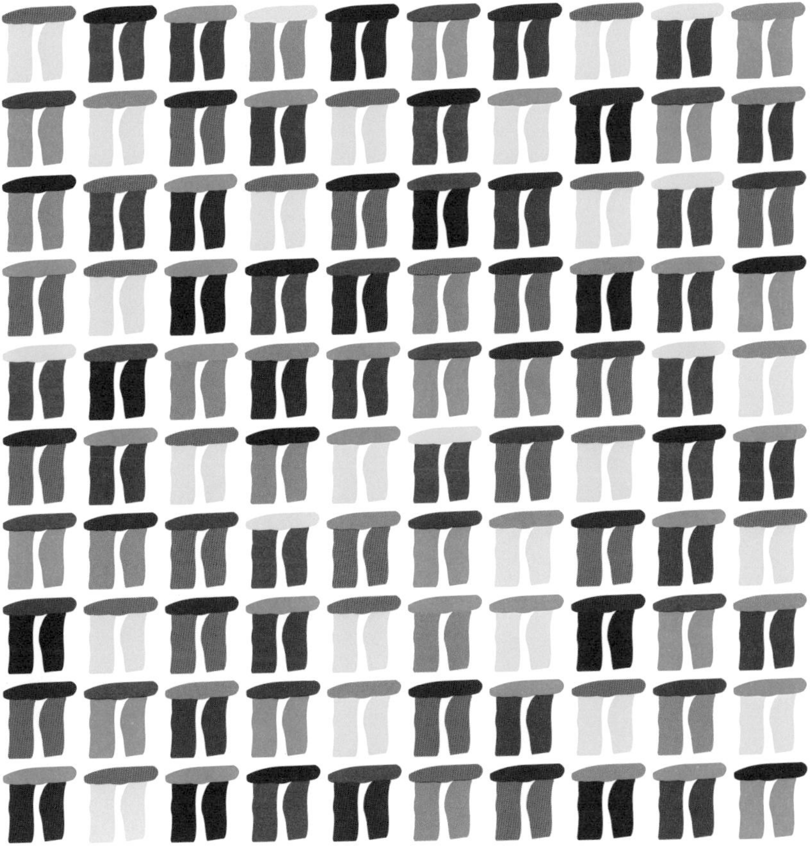

CREU·G·WIR·IN·THESE·STONES
FEL·GWYDR·HORIZONS
O·TH·WRNAIS·AWEN·SING

MILLENNIUM CENTRE CARDIFF

**TONIGHT ONLY!
THE STARS OF
WALES**

**TOM JONES
SHIRLEY BASSEY
BONNIE TYLER**

HOW MANY ALBUMS HAVE THE BEATLES SOLD IN THE USA?

A) 15 MILLION

B) 83 MILLION

C) 106 MILLION

THIS PAIR ONLY APPEARS ONCE
ON THE OPPOSITE PAGE

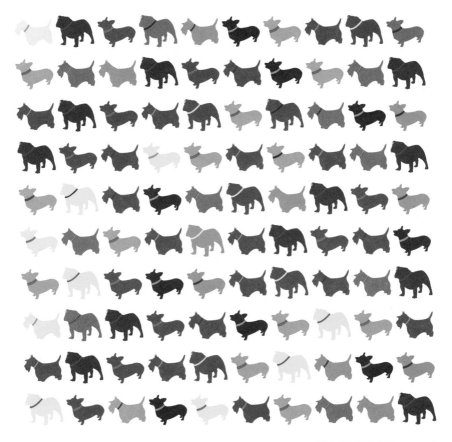

KNOW
BRITAIN?

FISH & CHIPS

WHICH DAY OF THE WEEK IS THE MOST POPULAR FOR EATING FISH AND CHIPS IN BRITAIN?

A) FRIDAY

B) SATURDAY

C) SUNDAY

BRITISH ISLANDS

SKYE
MULL
ANGLESEY
ISLAY
ARRAN
WIGHT
JURA
BUTE
SHEPPEY
HOLY
HAYLING
FOULNESS
LUNDY
THORNEY
BARDSEY

A	R	R	A	N	W	I	G	H	T
H	D	S	T	H	O	R	N	E	Y
A	B	J	K	O	J	U	R	A	E
Y	M	U	L	L	R	R	A	N	P
L	P	O	I	Y	L	L	B	G	P
I	Y	I	S	L	A	Y	U	L	E
N	D	S	G	K	R	E	T	E	H
G	N	F	O	U	L	N	E	S	S
J	U	D	R	E	S	K	Y	E	F
B	L	B	A	R	D	S	E	Y	K

FARMER DAI NEEDS TO CHECK ON HIS LEEKS!

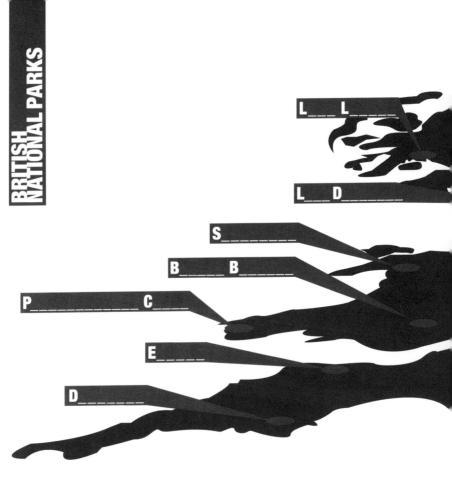

L_ _ _ L_ _ _ _

L_ _ _ _ D_ _ _ _ _ _ _

S_ _ _ _ _ _ _ _ _

B_ _ _ _ _ _ _ B_ _ _ _ _

P_ _ _ _ _ _ _ _ _ _ _ _ C_ _ _ _ _ _

E_ _ _ _ _

D_ _ _ _ _ _ _

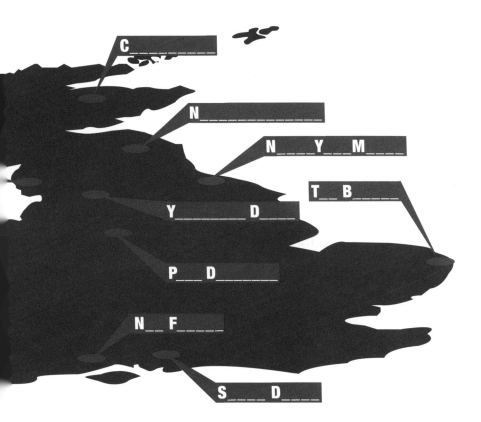

C_ _ _ _ _ _ _ _ _

N_ _ _ _ _ _ _ _ _ _ _

N_ _ Y_ _ M_ _ _ _

T_ _ B_ _ _ _ _ _

Y_ _ _ _ _ _ D_ _ _ _

P_ _ D_ _ _ _ _ _ _

N_ _ F_ _ _ _ _

S_ _ _ D_ _ _

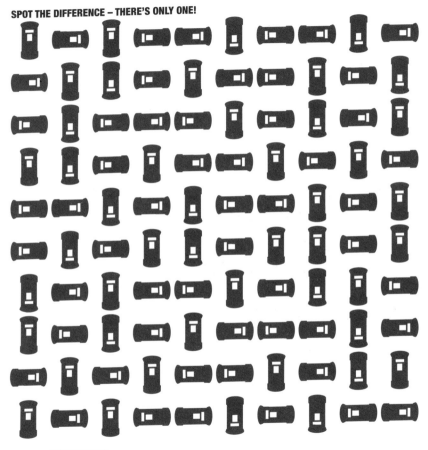

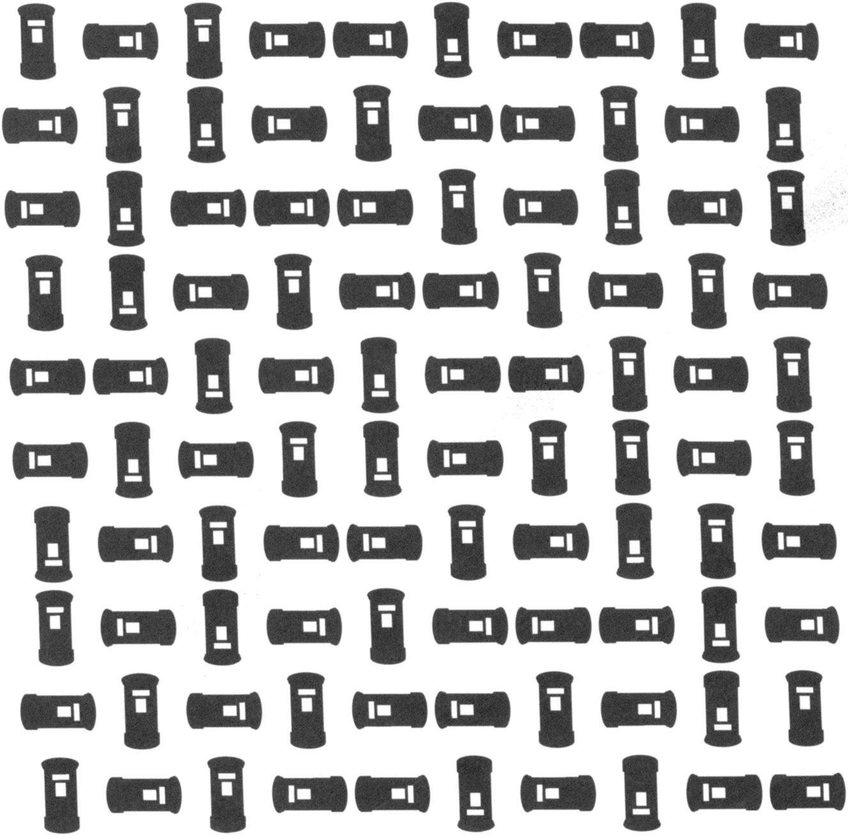

THIS PAIR ONLY APPEARS ONCE
ON THE OPPOSITE PAGE

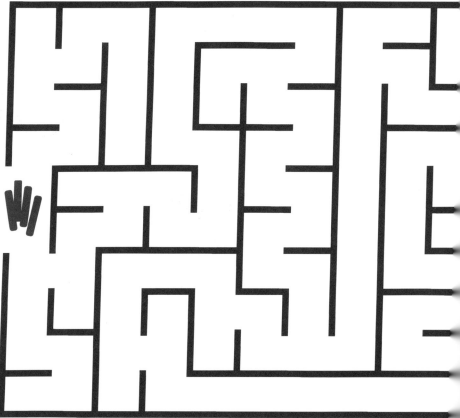

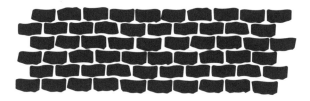

WHERE IS HADRIAN'S WALL?

A) ON THE SCOTTISH–ENGLISH BORDER

B) ON THE WELSH–ENGLISH BORDER

C) IN ENGLAND

THE NATIONAL COSTUME FOR THE WOMEN OF WALES IS BASED ON CLOTHES WORN BY:

A) SCHOOL HEADMISTRESSES FROM TOWNS ON THE ENGLISH-WELSH BORDER IN 1820

B) RURAL WOMEN IN WALES DURING THE NINETEENTH CENTURY

C) THE GRANDMOTHER OF KING WILLIAM IV

FIND THE 'GB' MINI

THIS PAIR ONLY APPEARS ONCE
ON THE OPPOSITE PAGE

ANSWERS

P4-5

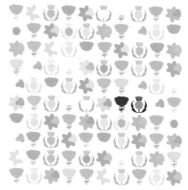

P6-7 A) A GIFT FOR HIS WIFE

P8-9

```
A B E R D E E N L M
C A L O N D O N G A
A N H X F U A E L N
M G R F F N E W A C
B O H O I D S P S H
R R T R D E N O G E
I O A D R E A R O S
D N B S A T W T W T
G N E W C A S T L E
E D I N B U R G H R
```

P10-11 C) ENGLISH ROSE, WELSH DAFFODIL, SCOTTISH THISTLE

P12-13

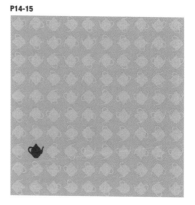

P14-15

P16-17

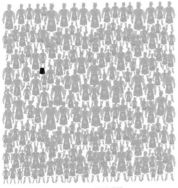

P18-19 B) A BOTTLE OF GORDON'S GIN

P20-21

P24-25

R	I	V	F	F	B	A	U	S	I
K	T	H	A	M	E	S	Y	P	G
C	R	L	Y	E	D	E	X	E	R
L	E	F	F	U	E	V	W	Y	E
Y	N	V	A	D	N	E	I	J	A
A	T	W	E	E	D	R	U	M	T
V	A	Y	N	E	F	N	V	B	O
O	Y	C	L	Y	D	E	M	E	U
N	L	T	A	F	F	N	T	R	S
W	E	R	T	Y	U	E	U	R	E

P26-27 C) WALES

MORE ANSWERS

P28-29

P30-31 A) 9

P32-33

P34-35 C) ANYWHERE SHE WISHES

P36-37

P38-39 C) AUSTRALIA

P40-41

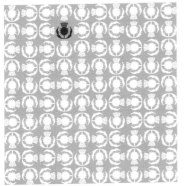

P42-43 C) 560,000

P44-45

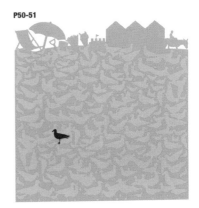

P46-47 A) BURIALS, GOOD FRIDAY AND CHRISTMAS

P48-49

P50-51

P52-53

P54-55 C) AS THE PASSWORD FOR THE HEADQUARTERS OF DILDANO IN THE MOVIE BARBARELLA

P58-59 B) EDIBLE

P56-57

P60-61

```
L I A T H A C H C G
L O C H N A G A R L
G O A T F E L L O Y
R S N O W D O N S D
A C A J K R W I S E
T A F A P E R G F R
C F Y U L A S D E F
B E N N E V I S L A
O L E H F P O I L W
R L P I K E W Y N R
```

P62-63

P 66–67 B) TEN TIMES AS MUCH

P68-69

P64-65

P70-71

P72-73 C) 106 MILLION

P74-75

P76-77 A) FRIDAY

P78-79

P80-81

A R R A N W I G H T
H D S T H O R N E Y Y
A B J K O J U R A E E
Y M U L L R R A N P P
L P O I Y L L B G P
I Y I S L A Y U L E
N D S G K R E T E H
G N F O U L N E S S
J U D R E S K Y E F
B L B A R D S E Y K

P82-83

P84-85

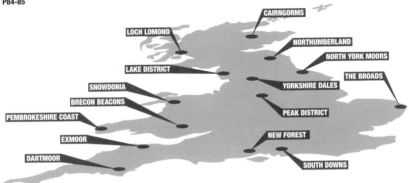

CAIRNGORMS

LOCH LOMOND

NORTHUMBERLAND

NORTH YORK MOORS

LAKE DISTRICT

THE BROADS

SNOWDONIA

YORKSHIRE DALES

BRECON BEACONS

PEAK DISTRICT

PEMBROKESHIRE COAST

EXMOOR

NEW FOREST

DARTMOOR

SOUTH DOWNS

P86-87

P88-89

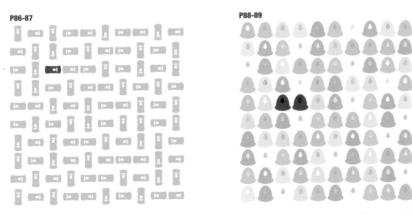

P90-91

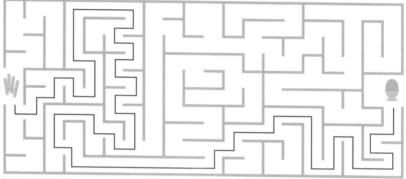

P92-93 C) IN ENGLAND

P94-95

P96-97 B) RURAL WOMEN IN WALES DURING THE NINETEENTH CENTURY

P98-99

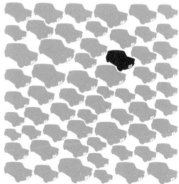

P100-101

IF YOU'RE INTERESTED IN FINDING OUT MORE ABOUT OUR BOOKS, FIND US ON FACEBOOK AT SUMMERSDALE PUBLISHERS AND FOLLOW US ON TWITTER AT @SUMMERSDALE.

WWW.SUMMERSDALE.COM

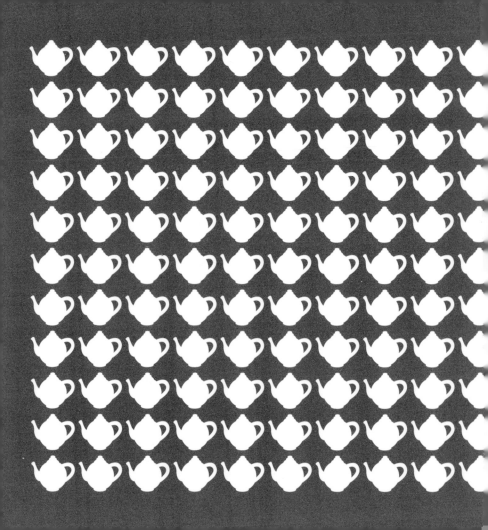